Permaculture for

*The Complete Beginners Crash Co
Permaculture Garden*

Copyright © 2015

All rights reserved. No part of this book may be reproduced in any form without permission in writing from the author. Reviewers may quote brief passages in reviews.

Disclaimer

No part of this publication may be reproduced or transmitted in any form or by any means, mechanical or electronic, including photocopying or recording, or by any information storage and retrieval system, or transmitted by email without permission in writing from the publisher.

While all attempts and efforts have been made to verify the information held within this publication, neither the author nor the publisher assumes any responsibility for errors, omissions, or opposing interpretations of the content herein.

This book is for entertainment purposes only. The views expressed are those of the author alone, and should not be taken as expert instruction or commands. The reader of this book is responsible for his or her own actions when it comes to reading the book.

Adherence to all applicable laws and regulations, including international, federal, state, and local governing professional licensing, business practices, advertising, and all other aspects of doing business in the US, Canada, or any other jurisdiction is the sole responsibility of the purchaser or reader.

Neither the author nor the publisher assumes any responsibility or liability whatsoever on the behalf of the purchaser or reader of these materials.

Any received slight of any individual or organization is purely unintentional.

Table of Contents

Introduction

Chapter 1 - Simplifying Permaculture

Chapter 2 - The Fundamental Principles

Chapter 3 - Small Spaces and Urban Homes Gardening

Chapter 4 - Making the Organic Garden

Chapter 5 - More Important Points to Ponder

Chapter 6 - What to Grow

Conclusion

Introduction

First and foremost I want to thank you for downloading the book, "Permaculture for Beginners – The Complete Beginners Crash Course Guide to Learning Permaculture Gardening for Life!"

In this book you will learn how to create a permaculture garden using limited resources and small spaces. You will also get to know the features of the natural ecology that your garden should exhibit.

If you are reading this book then you are one of those who aspire to grow their own foods, cultivate their own garden and do all these together with nature! Congratulations as you are having the efforts to contribute to changes and spread the Permaculture effect!

More than just a gardening strategy, a tool kit or a discipline, permaculture gardening is profound realization and sense of deep inner change to make a difference. You would want to be part of the solution instead of being part of the chaos.

Thanks again for downloading this book, I hope you enjoy it!

Chapter 1: Simplifying Permaculture

Do not be baffled when you hear the term permaculture. It is not a complex method of gardening hence, a straight forward, simple and essential tool for gardening and food growing alike. What most people know is that permaculture is a design system that has been present since the 70's. It is man's reaction to oil crisis and food insecurity. It involves the right attitude and practical application to become successful in gardening. Likewise it is a radical approach aiming quality food production.

The Evolution of Permaculture

Originally, this approach was developed by David Holmgren and Bill Mollison in the 1970's. Permaculture derives its name from the phrase "Permanent Culture" as both Mollison and Holmgren developed concepts to help human to come up with stable agriculture systems. Moreover, permaculture encourages the following concepts;

- The system was developed with the intention to create a well-balanced integration of the natural landscape and humans as it provides us food, materials for clothes and shelters and other essential materials and non-material things in a sustainable way.

- It provides design and maintenance of ecosystems that are agriculturally productive to have diversity, resilience and stability which are present in a natural ecosystem.

- The use of technology that only requires low energy inputs but provides high yields.

- The principles are applicable to both the rural and urban people to used.

Since then, permaculture has been constantly developed by other groups, organizations and even individuals across the globe and is now with multitude variety of approaches and standards but still has the same concept as above.

The modern-day permaculture approaches still integrate landscape, ecology, architecture, organic gardening and added agro-forestry in developing a sustainable and rich way of living.

Why Permaculture?

Permaculture's method is surrounded by reusing, recycling and regenerating of materials. Such were applied to gardening making it possible for us to grown foods anywhere we want to- from clay pots, to fences, to air and water, people now can produce higher yields without too much effort and resources by just adopting nature's way.

Furthermore permaculture aims for natural growing system that is sustainable in a continuous cycle unlike most of the modern agricultural methods. This way of gardening also seeks to turn the food wastes into something valuable, replace artificial weed killers with the natural predators, recreate the whole cycle and have a natural composition mimicking that of the nature. Hence, permaculture gardening is one with the nature and not to be against it.

The Ethics

The ethics that form the basis for developing permaculture includes *being fair, caring for people and caring for Earth*. These ethics support the idea that people can come up with systems wherein both the planet and its inhabitants can attain the state of well-being and keeping the balance at the same time. Simply think of it this way- natural resources should not be merely dissipate for personal profit and in a way that it can lead to destruction and depletion of the natural ecosystems.

Permaculture is a vast, holistic approach that consists of a myriad of applications. At the center of all these sustainable designs and systems, there are set of fundamental cores, values, practices and applications which remain constant regardless of the changes and development. As a beginner, we will discuss the basics of permaculture and how you could actually benefit from it.

The Best Option

Unfortunately, innovations and advancements in gardening technology tend to be very unsustainable and destructive for the world's natural resources in the long run. Such are detrimental to land; people, plants and animals' survival hence, following the permaculture way will enable us to still have our basic needs without exploiting, degrading and abusing the natural resources. Not only permaculture and its disciplines can help us to develop agricultural systems, it also can aid us in enhancing the way we build our homes in terms of design and architecture. Various communities were now composed of low impact homes. Nonetheless, permaculture has more to offer to improve our quality of living.

Understanding the multiple functions of every element in the garden will help you become successful in your permaculture gardening. Later on this book you will learn how each elements function and complement one another and mutually benefits others. Unfortunately, many gardeners are still stuck with the conventional type of gardening and does not want to take advantage of the myriad of benefits that permaculture has to offer.

Furthermore permaculture is teaching us how to conserve our energy, money and time by looking creatively to the resources that we already have. It also wants us to take advantage of whatever situation we have now (no backyard, living in an apartment, etc) and to use the situation to our advantage.

What we like best about permaculture principle is that it is applicable not only with gardening but with other human's aspect of life. Such is that we have to see the good in every situation and turn the problems into solutions.

Chapter 2: The Fundamental Principles

When developing your permaculture garden, the focus should be on planting native flowers, trees and fruits. Preferably the things that are native within the area which require less water. Again our goal here is to work with nature rather than working against it. Usually, permaculture systems has at least 3 purposes. For an instance, corn stalk produces corn and this could also be used in growing some climbing beans which can be used in feeding the cattle.

There are fundamental permaculture principles you should consider before you actually turn your garden into a system that is sustainable.

Energy Efficiency - the first and one of the important things to look for is the situation of your house. Energy efficiency is key when you are planning for the garden design. Simply, put your veggie or herb garden near the kitchen back door so it will be easier for you to harvest those tomatoes or pick those mint leaves. The area should be closest to your house and each zone must be identified. The furthest zone should be the area that you can visit least.

Zoning is vital so you could be more productive with your gardening. Find out which area or zone would tend to be the busiest, what plants or herbs require frequent watering or tending and which of your plants have to be placed nearest the house.

Maximize - maximize your land and find out how to take advantage of it; where does the sun rises and sets? This information will help you decide on the ideal spot for you to place your food garden. Is the wind prevailing in the easter part? Maybe you will need a windbreaker growing on the area. Are there any shaded and sheltered spots to use? Knowing these basic essentials would aid you in deciding better for your garden.

Likewise, make sure to maximize structures and tools that you will place in your garden. Some architectural tools like as a trellis can be used in training vines or to block strong winds.

Diversity - another principle of permaculture gardening is to grow a diverse range of herbs, food plants or flowers exhibiting mutual relationships with each other. Carefully choose the plants to include in your garden and as much as possible, include native varieties as these plants require less attention and maintenance. By doing such, gardeners will be able to have maximum gain with a minimal input.

Everything should be natural - another permaculture principle is for people to use organic materials. The system encourages production of organic vegetables, livestock and fruits. Thus, soil must be fed with compost, seaweed, wood ash, liquid manures and other natural materials rather using insecticides and pesticides. Everything should be recycled and put back in the soil. Instead of using artificial and chemical fertilizers, you can grow Nitrogen-fixing cover crops to add nitrogen to your soil. Fish meal, raw sugar and blood and bone wastes can be sued for adding phosphates to it.

Recycle it all – grass clippings to be added in the compost bin, vegetable scraps and soft woods for the ducks and chickens, prunings and hardwood cutting to be put on a mulching machine and used throughout the garden to encourage water pretension.

Now it is clear to you that permaculture gardening is more than just the usual organic gardening. This system aims for sustainable planting and growing while working with ecology. Hence, trying the permaculture way of gardening also means trying to create a garden where everything is co-dependent and dependent with each other.

Permaculture has many features and these could be learned by searching on the internet or enrolling yourself to a permaculture course. There are also online communities that can help you in learning the basic of the systems.

Where to Start

You can start permaculture gardening in your own garden or backyard however, if you don't have one, a balcony garden or a patio can be productive as well. How about community gardening? There are community programs where you can adopt a certain plot and grow your plants there. Design is one of the most essential things you must learn in permaculture as it is a multidisciplinary design system. However, making your first step is usually the hardest.

The first step is for you to figure out what exactly a permaculture garden is for you. You have to think of various ideas and picture out what type of garden you would want to create. With a finalized design, you have something to develop and putting those ideas in a paper will ensure your commitment to it. Vague ideas could only lead you to procrastinating.

A concrete and highly practical philosophy, permaculture offers strategies and various design principles so you could come up with regenerative and at the same time, resilient system.

Moreover, the strategies and design principles are applicable to a wide range of permaculture gardening however; we will discuss the primary design principles for outdoor living systems and landscapes.

Key Principle Designs

Thoughtful observation – this includes learning about the topography, history, soil conditions, movement of water and wind, sunlight patterns, ecology and human involvement also known as sector analysis. This is of utmost importance if you are aiming for significant changes as errors could be committed in your design if you will neglect these factors.

Determine a yield – yield simply means any product that you can obtain from a system. For an instance, material yields include water, food, and energy, building materials, clothing, medicine, paper and fibre while non-material yields include learning, aesthetics, recreation, community and added income. The good thing about nature is that it increasingly becomes productive over time.

Small steps – usually, the best and well-praised permaculture designs are those who started small. After affirmation, it then scaled-up and becomes one of the most efficient designs. Small changes could offer the greatest effects so don't start with a large scale design to save you time and effort.

Multiple functions – the elements in your design must serve more than one function. Realize that everything you see in nature has multiple functions as they are included in a myriad of relationships, doing various services. For example, a well-placed tree could provide shade, food, beauty, bio-mass, cooling, building materials and structure for other plants to use. It can also serve as habitat for small animals and insects and serves as recreation for people.

Multiple services – this principle promotes resiliency and less fragility. Various strategies could be implemented to sustain water needs for the garden such as high soil organic matter, household grey water use, landscape contour or roof-top catchment in addition to the usual water sources you have. Ti better support food production's key elements, you could also use different growing models like edible perennials, forest gardens, annual vegetable beds, small livestock such as rabbits and chicken.

Stacking in space and time – normally we would want to grow as much as possible plants or flowers in a vertical plane. This is to maximize as well the food, bio-mass and other yields we can generate from the system. Hence you could create wall mounted systems, multi-layered planting areas, green roofs and espaliered fruit trees.

There's no end as to where you can apply these permaculture designs, whether you are in the crowded city or in a town with vast landscapes available. Your creativity, willingness to learn and knowledge about permaculture gardening will help you to get started growing your own foods.

Chapter 3: Small Spaces and Urban Homes Gardening

Some people who gained interest with permaculture gardening tend to get disappointed easily upon realizing that their space is very limited and have various urban environment constraints. Fortunately regardless if you are living in an urban setting or in a high-rise condo, you could still enjoy the benefits and beauty of permaculture gardening.

Designing permaculture garden can be challenging as one is not only applying organic gardening techniques but also applying a tool kit and decision-making skills for properly developing sustainable human settlements.

The Problem Can Also be the Solution

Most of us are living in small, urban spaces which limit our access to actual soil. Most gardening and permaculture books present images of abundant farm landscapes and vast suburban lots with overflowing fruits, tress, greenery, some small livestock and vegetable gardens. These scenarios made us feel frustrated living in n apartments or just having a small sized yard near the front door.

Fortunately you can do a lot despite the fact that you don't have a huge land to begin with. Another popular principle of permaculture is turning the problems into solutions. The usual restraints in an urban setting include density of people, buildings and resources. The latter can be used for your advantage since you can acquire solar exposure, vertical growing or intensive planting you can actually do indoors. Below are some useful ideas you can adopt.

APARTMENT DWELLINGS

Look for windows where you can get decent sun exposure and create a beautiful window garden. There are hydroponic window farm strategies you can try which only require no soil and minimum space. Others are creative in using plastic bottles as well. Other spaces such as fire escapes, stoops and balconies are also perfect areas for container gardens.

Moreover it will be easier for you to harvest the yield and use such in your kitchen. Make sure to place the containers where maximum sunlight exposure is available. You can also purchase self-watering planter boxes for a more manageable garden.

Consider various types of Growing

Contrary to what most people think, not all types of gardening require green leaves and soil especially if you are growing food. For an instance, you can learn how to grow gourmet mushrooms using the bucket method. There are also kits available online where you can use in creating a compact garden that can be placed in the bathroom or in the kitchen counter.

Likewise, you can enjoy growing live cultures also known as fermenting. It is another form of growing food. You could also try vermicomposting. A form of gardening which can also help in getting rid with kitchen scraps.

Find other ways to plant

Discover other ways of growing food beyond your apartment's area like engaging in community gardens. Other options could be growing on other's backyards with their permission, on median strips, rooftop beekeeping or rooftop gardening.

SMALL YARDS

Even if your front yard or back yard is small, you can still make the most out of it by using strategies such as bio-intensive gardening and square-foot gardening. These strategies will help you maximize your yields even with a small area. One popular permaculture gardening strategy is called keyhole garden beds. This will aid you in maximizing your growing space while minimizing the path space. If you are aiming on growing fruit trees against fences and walls, there are high density pruning and espalier techniques you can apply.

Place them strategically

Although the neighbour's house is too close with yours, you can still make use the front or back space of the yard. Trellises help in saving space and you can also create fun projects with it. When placed accordingly, the trellis can serve as protection for the plants. Living wall planters and wall garden are other effective methods in growing vertically at aesthetically pleasing at the same time.

To effectively produce yields and be able to grow healthy crops in a permaculture garden, one must acquire proper learning. Some research and interviews with other permaculture gardeners will help. Whilst it takes some efforts, you can be assured to gain long-term pay-off. You will experience the benefits of permaculture gardening without exerting too much effort and resources. Make use of the available spaces at home and start creating you "little" garden.

Fortunately, the principles of permaculture gardening can work anywhere, any scale and in any climate. These principles and designs are applicable to housing estates to the whole village, or to a small front yard and balcony to a vast backyard. Start with the walls in your balcony or patio. Others find it handy to use plastic bottles. Be resourceful and creative as well. Anything goes with permaculture garden as long as you are working together with nature.

Think ahead of the designs and plan your permaculture garden accordingly. This won't take much effort on your part and can mostly look after itself if things are in their right places. Read other related books, journals and sources for the internet. This will expand your knowledge on various permaculture gardens and how you could implement such designs.

Chapter 4: Making the Organic Garden

In any natural habitat, plants, animals and other micro-organisms work harmoniously to keep the balance of the ecology. As with organic permaculture, incorporating insects, both predators and pests is helpful to maintain the balance of the loop.

On the contrary, people use pesticides in getting rid of the insect pests. The more these pests multiply, the more we apply strong pesticides. In the case of organic permaculture gardening, there's no need to use pesticides. These chemicals will only make the pests immune thus, stronger applications of it becomes inevitable.

In a permaculture garden, there is balance. No need for pesticides as preys and predators are in a balanced loop with insects, animals and plants. And once it has established, we also need not to do anything but plant, water, mulch and harvest the yields.

The Composition

Soil - although we are designing a no-dig organic permaculture garden, we still need some soil to start with. To obtain long-term success of the garden we have to make sure that there is enough sunlight exposure, protection and adequate enrichment present in our soil.

Worm farms - although these are not a critical item needed in a permaculture garden, worms when placed with castings, liquid produces and compost are essential in keeping the vitality of the soil and its health. Moreover it can also help in removing vegetable scraps, weeds, old newspapers and animal manures.

Chickens - manures of organically raised chickens are high in essential elements such as nitrogen and other minerals for the soil. Moreover chickens can clean-up garden pests if you allowed them to roam.

Chicken shed - in making your chicken shed, put chicken bedding by mixing straws and Lucerne hay. Use materials that are snake-proof as well to avoid your chicken being eaten by snakes living in the garden. At least 5-7 chickens will suffice a 20-square meter block but you can add more but no more than 10. Create two openings in a separate direction. This will enable you to free your chicken to roam in a direction away from the vegetable sections especially if you are still establishing the seedlings.

The chicken's diet mainly consists of worms and insects thus, you can be sure that there will be few pests, you will have a healthy soil and of course, a regular supply of pesticide-free eggs.

Compost heaps - are vital in an organic permaculture garden as it helps in utilizing organic materials that tend to be discarded. Remember that in a permaculture garden, one of the design principles is not to waste anything organic and recycle it. Chicken bedding, grass clippings and vegetable scraps can be put together in compost and come up with rich compost for your soil. However do not include meat scraps as these will only attract vermin.

Water - this is a very important element in most forms of gardening to avoid getting the plants and soil dehydrated.

Water tends to attract native birds and other insects too. If you want to encourage frogs, wasps and dragon flies, have your water feature combined with some mud.

Depending on the soil's quality, a deep soak is typically needed prior to cultivation. Your watering system must be laid out and set up completely onto the soil and lawn. After the soil is well-watered, fork it especially the vegetable beds for better water penetration.

Habitats and covers- logs, small rocks and water feature can be the ideal place for pests and predators to live like frogs, lizards, spiders and small snakes. Although some of us wouldn't welcome the idea of having snakes or spiders in their garden, these creatures are playing an important role in closed loop system. They can aid in keeping vermin and other pests at bay.

Remember that the levels of predators and pests must be kept healthy all the time. If the pests has turned to be more populated or the predators become out of hand, perhaps there is something missing in your garden. Deal with it and determine the missing link without using harmful pesticides.

For added protection to other elements, putting some screening plants will help. Likewise they will attract more insects and birds however, ensure sure that your screening plants are not directly blocking the sunlight.

Additional Tips

- When preparing the vegetable beds, generously apply compost and covered it heavily with mulch.

- As the vegetable bed matures, you can have it turn it over. This will allow the seeds to be directly planted in the soil and grow even before the next mulching.

- Monocultures can be present especially if you are growing corn in a bed but you can address through cross fertilization. Planting onions, tomato, garlic and other herbs will also help in keeping the diversity of the bed.

- Considerate first solar orientation before placing your seedlings or start gardening. Lands facing south will get abundant sun exposure while it's vice-versa for lands facing the north.

- Earth works and swales (hollow area) should be worked ahead of time before the actual planting of bushes or fruit trees. Making swales to the terrain and other changes to it can help prevent flooding. You can also create water catchment and divert the supply of water directly to the garden.

- Use gravity whenever possible especially for heavy bulk items. For an instance, the water should flow according to gravity or else, you will need to rely on electric pumps to improve water flow to your garden. Likewise if the supply of water is higher than the garden, less labor will be needed in watering the plants.

Place your water catchment at elevated spots or use structures to make it possible. Let gravity pull down the water for better irrigation system. This is w win-win situation since you will have lighter work to do.

-Varied and mixed gardens are highly recommended since this setting rarely gets a foothold of diseases. There are bugs and pest that can only identify the plants by their look thus, mixing your cabbages with onion, flowers and other herbs will prevent the pest and the diseases form spreading as this is only possible with related plants.

- Since pests are very specific in the plant that they like, raising the same type of plants together in a certain area would mean a big feast for the pests. Diseases can also spread spontaneously. This is why permaculture design promotes variety and diversity which is the exact opposite with conventional gardening. Doing this will help you avoid problems relating to infestations and associated issues.

One of the hardest tasks in developing a permaculture garden is to start its actual construction. It may take you weeks and even months to finalize you designs and still have doubts and questions when beginning the project. Remember that things will be more manageable when you have them in smaller tasks. Likewise, motivation is needed so you could overcome any delays, obstacles and problems you may encounter while creating your organic permaculture garden.

Chapter 5: More Important Points to Ponder

Still getting confused about permaculture gardening? Simply, any garden, regardless of its size and compositions, as long as it emulates pattern same with of the nature, is considered a permaculture garden. Now, the degree of permaculture principles present in your design is the thing that you should have to decide at the outset.

The size of your garden could be from a container in the balcony to vast food forest. Determine the amount of "permaculture" you wish to achieve and whether if your garden is similar with the traditional veggie garden with a little permaculture design principles or a full-scale food forest complete with stacking, edge and other elements. Then, decide on which of the design principles you want to use and to what degree do you want it to emphasize. Similarly, find out how your garden emulates nature by trying to answer these questions.

How do you want to protect the garden's soil?

- Through mulching, place some ground cover plants and other ways

- maintaining bare soil means working against nature since nature wanted to fill it with things that will serve as its protection thus, weeds come handy

- Bare soil can be easily eroded by rain, degrading its structure and can wash away its top layer

-The no-dig design aims to preserve the soil. Turning the soil more often can also destroy its structure while exposing the deepest layer to heat and sun's UV rays which can be harmful for the composition of the soil.

- make adequate size of garden beds so you can easily reach for them without stepping on the beds. Garden beds are efficient in keeping the soil healthy. Take note that stepping on it can prevent water and air penetration on the roots of the plants which will affect their health and reduces their productivity.

What are the soil building activities you can make to repair the soil that is already dead, compacted, damaged or has very little organic content?

- Use plants like dandelions and fenugreek or any plants that has deep tap roots to help break the soil

- If necessary, try digging or forking the ground once to loosen the soil then mulch it and cover it

- Using compost can bring life and health to the soil. Use compost heaps or apply other composting techniques

- Green manures are also effective to used in mulching the soil as these add nitrogen

- Again, do not step on the garden beds. Put some earthworms in the soil to do the digging and avoid digging the soil unless extremely necessary

Do Some Zone Planning

Zoning is important in the traditional permaculture design. It is composed of 5 zones. Zone 0 will serve as your house; it should be the center of the whole system. Furthermore, this area is where the action will start.

Next, your zone 1 should be the area nearest to the house. This is where you will put all the components that requires human attention such as organic material bins and and the garden.

Zone 3 would be the actual vegetable beds or where the plants will grow and be harvested. Zone 4 is where you can manage woodlands and produced lumber. Lastly, zone 5 represents the wilderness. It would be last and farthest zone from zone 0, your house as this area is self-sustaining and can manage without adequate attention from you.

One with Nature

In practice, you don't actually need to replicate the design of a natural ecosystem rather, it is more of the application of it basic principles which matter. No one tends, fertilizes, remove weeds or sprays pesticides in the forest but the forest is still able to produce fruits, nuts, building materials, paper, medicinal herbs and other essential needs of mankind. Thus, permaculture is more of mimicking the natural system like that of the forest to obtain a productive yield without doing too much work.

Design is Key

As various principles of permaculture covers human's important life aspects, humans in return can do so much to enhance their relationship with nature. Developing an organic garden and understanding the animals and plants live, aid us in being more concern and mindful of life's abundance and importance.

Think about it, the forest can grown and produce various materials and non-material things but nobody digs, plants, remove weeds or take care of the trees. Thus permaculture gardening is teaching us how to adopt the nature's strategy. It has its own, natural solution that a gardener might possible experience in their gardens.

Moreover nature is an ultimate recycler as everything goes on and on with it. Everything and every living creatures are resources and there's no thing as waste to it. Sustainability is something that works in the long run. With the right design of garden, the proper arrangement of elements and the function of one another, you garden could produce more yields without you doing all the hard work.

Chapter 6: What to Grow?

Nowadays, you really don't have a clue whether the food you are eating are safe whilst you purchase it from a high-end grocery or food shop. Likewise we also want to acquire healthy foods without breaking the family budget. One efficient action that growers see is for people to grow their own foods. There are many convincible reasons why you must consider growing your own food even in your windowsill, in a small yard or even in the patio.

Talking about permaculture plants, these are popular plants that is widely used in permaculture designs. They support the aim for sustainable gardening and helps you create a garden that requires little resources. Hence, a timely, thriving garden that looks after itself.

Pesticide-Free Foods

The used of commercial pesticides has increased by almost 600% according to a study. Similarly, mixed salads bags you can buy in the market are usually washed with chloride to prolong its shelf life. Such practices are hardly healthy eating for the whole family.

Hence, growing your own food and purchasing locally produced fruits and vegetables are the greenest things you can do for the family, community and nature.

Select What Foods to Grow

Engaging your whole family in permaculture gardening sounds fun and the one of the exciting part for this is selecting the kind of foods you wanted to grow. Use organic seeds of fruits and vegetables that your children or relatives like to eat. Usually, a strawberry bed is a must but you can also have alpine strawberries in the garden.

Fruits and Vegetables

Vegetables such as parsnips, sweet corn, spinach, bush beans, carrots and cherry tomatoes are among the most convenient for starters. Likewise these foods can be incorporated in many different dishes. Self-seeding salads such as land cress and oak leaf lettuces are also recommended for beginners to try. A small bed of salad can help you save for a week's budget while making sure that you and your family are eating organic foods.

Kids also love harvesting so it is a good way to bond with them. Hence you are also able to teach them the importance of knowing where their food comes from.

Herbs

Other people prefer to grow herbs in their permaculture gardens. Whilst you can derive many benefits from planting fruits and veggies, growing herbs also aid in creating a healthy garden as herbs help in fertilization. They also tend to attract pollinators and other essential elements and at the same time, can prevent pests. Below are some of the most useful herbs you can try growing in your garden

Dandelions- while other considers this plant as a harmful weed, dandelions have various benefits for the garden such as fertilizer. They can reach the subsoil with their long, taproots and can dredge essential nutrients from it. Then they will store the nutrients in their leaves. When the leaves where cut back or died and decomposed, it can fertilize the soil.

Fennel – is a strong-scented herb which is normally paired with basil in a growing landscape. The flowers of it are beneficial for insects and other pollinators. Having fennels in your garden will attract various insects such as butterflies, hoverflies and ladybugs. However keep your fennels at the edge of the garden as not all plant can grow along well with it. Likewise fennels are good in accumulating phosphorus.

Chamomile – you can do so many things with chamomile but one of its best features is that it acts as a physician to the other plants. Any plant next to it can be healed. Also, the roots of chamomile tend to dredge up calcium, potassium and phosphorous. It said to enhance growth of onions and cabbage crops and grows well under fruit trees.

Chives- are another common herb which is very useful in the kitchen. Its leaves and flowers are good to make an edible garnish in salads and other dishes. Like the chamomile, chives are plant fertilizer and accumulate calcium and potassium. Pollinators can also get easily attracted and the chives' scent is unpleasing for pests.

Moreover this herb is also said to repel fruit tree diseases and pests hence planting a ring of it near your tress will be helpful.

Characteristics of Plants Ideal for Permaculture Garden

Aside the plants and herbs mentioned above below are other characteristics of permaculture plants to use as basis in selecting the type of plants to grow.

- Perennials are a favorite since they create permanent system versus the annual plants

- Pioneer plants or those that can live under harsh conditions such as poor soil. Likewise these plants require little attention and can enhance their growing area to make it suitable to other plants

- Legumes are also recommended since they are helpful in converting nitrogen from the air to soil nitrogen to be used by other plants.

- Deep-rooted plants can dig the subsoil for nutrients. When its leaves were cut or dropped in the soil, the nutrients will be deposited on top of it. Hence it becomes mulch and can feed shallow rooted plants when it breaks down. They can also break through clay pans and hardened layers which improves the subsoil layers that vegetables cannot penetrate.

- Rather than buying mulch, there are some plants that can be used for mulch. They even grow and serve as living mulch. These type of plants have the capability to keep the soils' moist, compete with weeds for nutrients and increase the soil's organic matter content.

These are some examples perhaps, the most typically used permaculture plants. There are more plants that can benefit your permaculture system such as fodder plants, edible plants and medicinal plants. You could try using and experimenting with them. However focus on plants that can benefit your soil and other plants as it is the foundation of having a thriving and sustainable garden. And of course, this depends on how you would want to use the plants in your garden. Discover the multiple functions these plants can offer and put them into use.

More Ideas for Gardening

Stacking – this method allows gardeners to grow several types of crops that get along well in the same bed. This is efficient for those who have limited areas to plant with. Likewise the crops will be able to support and give each other protection from pests and shade from direct sunlight.

Companion – similar with stacking, companion planting also allows you to grow similar crops or crops that complement each other. If one crop will be affected by pests and bugs, the other crops will confuse it by their shapes and scents, preventing the whole crops getting a foothold. This method of gardening also promotes resiliency, stimulates plant growth and attract beneficial insects.

Animals and fishes - these are commonly raised in a permaculture garden since they can add beauty and have function in maintaining the balance of the ecology. Chickens can produce eggs and meat while their manure serve as rich fertilizer.

Edging - this is the most productive of any ecosystem as the environment transforms. To emphasize this principle you could choose to lean towards the curved edges of the beds or use smaller rectangular beds.

Vertical gardening - another ideal type of gardening that you can do even in a small space is vertical gardening. Some vines like passion fruit, kiwi fruit and grapes can be grown over structures such as fences, pergolas, trellises, and arches. Watermelons, pumpkins, rock melons, zucchini, gourds and loofahs can also be vertically grown using wire mesh and supported posts.

Water gardens - apparently aquatic ecosystems play a vital role in any ecosystem designs. These can be used in growing edible aquatic plants like lotus, chestnuts, Vietnamese mints and Sagittarian. It can also support amphibious and aquatic life such as frogs and fishes. If the pond is also spacious enough, it can manage ducks.

Managing all the interconnecting systems will make you a leader. Once all the areas are connected and working in your garden, you have to make sure that they will stay balance and finely working together. Add compost as needed, get rid of pests, monitor your crops and plants, protect the animals in the garden and apply the principles of permaculture to become successful in your gardening.

Nonetheless, having a permaculture garden of your own is a rewarding task. Other types and kinds of fruits, vegetables and herbs can actually try growing depending on your preferences.

Your garden (regardless how huge or small it is), is the great place for you to experiment and try various permaculture designs. The experience is the most efficient teacher. Likewise it's not important if your garden is well-established or not. A motivated and creative gardener can always enhance it over time.

Conclusion

Thank you again for downloading this book!

I hope this book was able to help you to fully understand the basic principles and designs of permaculture gardening and how it can actually benefit you and the community.

The next step upon successful completion of this book is to plan and design your own permaculture garden. Remember that more than being sustainable and having good resources of our everyday needs, permaculture gardens promotes great lifestyle change. Its principles are promoting nature's rules and ways.

You see, in a conventional garden, you or the gardener will be the one to satisfy all the garden's necessities. With permaculture gardening, you are to apply nature's way hence, you will only do minimal works and other repetitive tasks can be taken off by the garden itself. A bit smarter right? Thus you can save more resources and energy while still expecting to obtain higher yields.

I hope that this book will be your constant reminder and reference on your goal of achieving a sustainable permaculture garden. Happy gardening!

Finally, if you enjoyed this book, please take the time to share your thoughts and post a review on Amazon. It'd be greatly appreciated!

Thank you and good luck!

Printed in Great Britain
by Amazon